IN HISTORY
WARFARE

Authors:

David Smith and Derek Newton

Illustrated by Melvyn K. Powell

SCHOFIELD & SIMS LTD., HUDDERSFIELD

First impression 1971

©1971 Schofield & Sims Ltd.
0 7217 1538 9
0 7217 1568 0   Net edition

Printed in England by Stott Bros. Ltd., Halifax.

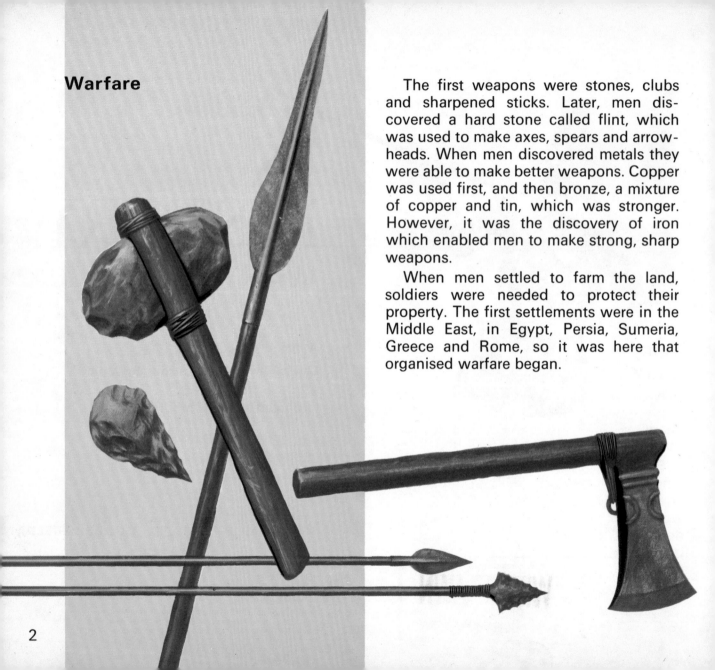

Warfare

The first weapons were stones, clubs and sharpened sticks. Later, men discovered a hard stone called flint, which was used to make axes, spears and arrowheads. When men discovered metals they were able to make better weapons. Copper was used first, and then bronze, a mixture of copper and tin, which was stronger. However, it was the discovery of iron which enabled men to make strong, sharp weapons.

When men settled to farm the land, soldiers were needed to protect their property. The first settlements were in the Middle East, in Egypt, Persia, Sumeria, Greece and Rome, so it was here that organised warfare began.

Sumeria

The Sumerians lived on the fertile plain between the River Tigris and the River Euphrates. Their chief weapon was the war chariot, which was very heavy and was pulled by two or four asses.

Each chariot had a driver, and a warrior armed with a javelin and a spear. As the chariot raced towards the enemy the warrior hurled his javelin before jumping down to use his spear. With the discovery of the spoked wheel chariots became faster and lighter, so they were pulled by horses. By 2000 B.C. the warrior carried a bow with which he shot arrows with flint arrowheads. The Sumerians also used maces and copper axes.

Phalanx

Footsoldiers were organised into groups, each called a phalanx. Each soldier carried a large shield and a long spear. The phalanx fought shoulder to shoulder in six ranks. At first the Sumerians wore leather helmets, but these were later replaced by copper ones. Some warriors wore body armour. This was a long cloak which had pieces of metal fastened to it.

Ancient Egypt

The power of the Egyptian army was its bowmen, who had a powerful composite bow made of wood, animal horn, sinews and glue, all stuck together. The Egyptian charioteers charged the enemy while the warriors threw javelins or fired their bows. On the side of the chariot was a quiver with spare arrows or javelins in it. These warriors fought from the chariots all the time, but the Egyptian army also had many footsoldiers who used spears or bows. For a long time Egyptian warriors wore no body armour, but they did wear a leather helmet and carried a large shield.

Later, the bowmen and charioteers, who

needed both hands free, wore body armour. This was a linen tunic covered with plates of metal.

All cities had strong walls to protect them, but now migdols or square forts were built to protect important places such as main roads or walls. Attackers had to climb the walls with scaling ladders or breach the walls with battering rams. If the walls were too thick or too high then the attackers surrounded the strongpoint and tried to starve out the defenders.

5

Assyria

The Assyrians had soldiers mounted on horses. Some were bowmen while others were spearmen. Mounted spearmen opened the attack, followed by spearmen on foot. The bowmen kept on the edge of the battle, pouring arrows at the enemy. They usually operated in pairs. One carried a bow while the other carried a large shield to protect them both. The Assyrian army also contained slingers. Each Assyrian soldier wore a metal helmet and a long tunic which reached down to his ankles. The tunic was covered with strips of metal or bone. Every soldier had a long iron sword.

The Assyrians also used chariots which were heavier than Egyptian chariots and sometimes contained four men.

Siege Weapons

Assyrians were experts at siege warfare. They had huge six-wheeled battering rams. While the battering rams beat against the walls, spearmen attacked with scaling ladders. Behind them archers and slingers poured a devastating fire at the defenders. If the walls were very high or very thick, the Assyrians tunnelled under them to make them collapse.

Catapult

Scaling platform

Ancient Greece

The most successful Greek army was led by Alexander the Great. His main army consisted of three parts — the cavalry, called the companions, the hypaspists, an élite body of footsoldiers, and the hoplites or spearmen. Both hypaspists and hoplites used long spears and swords. They fought in a dense formation called a phalanx. Each spearman wore a breastplate, leg guards called greaves, and a large plumed helmet which covered all his face except his eyes. He also carried a small shield.

The Greek army also had its archers and javelin men.

Alexander used his phalanx to check the enemy while he launched his superb cavalry. To capture walled cities he had scaling towers, rams and catapults. Small catapults hurled arrows, javelins, or stones weighing almost four kilogrammes, while bigger catapults hurled stones with a mass of up to twenty-five kilogrammes. If necessary his sappers tunnelled under the walls.

Ancient Rome

The Legion

The strength of the Roman army was its footsoldiers who were divided up into legions of about six thousand men. Each legion was split into ten cohorts, each cohort into six centuries, and each century into ten contubernia. In command of each century was a centurion. The emblem of a legion was its eagle. Each group of ten men did its own cooking.

The legionary usually enlisted for twenty years. He was armed with a short, stabbing sword and a javelin, and he carried a shield made of leather and wood. Its edges were bound with metal strips, and it had a leather handgrip. His helmet was made of bronze or iron.

There were four types of body armour:
1. A leather tunic.
2. A leather tunic with metal plates sewn on it.
3. Chain mail which was made by linking metal rings together.
4. Lorica which was made of bands of metal which circled the body and crossed over the shoulders.

In battle the legionaries stood in two or three ranks, shoulder to shoulder, protected by their shields. As they approached the enemy they threw their javelins and then attacked with their swords.

The Testudo

To protect themselves from missiles hurled at them, the Romans had a battle formation called the testudo. The front rank held their shields in front, while the other ranks held their shields above their heads so that the group of soldiers looked like a huge tortoise.

The Romans had a wide variety of siege equipment, including many catapults which fired stone balls, arrows or even lead bullets.

The Roman army was finally defeated by the Goth and Hun horsemen. These horsemen had a valuable piece of equipment, the stirrup. This helped them to retain their seat in the saddle while using their weapons. The Goths used fearsome, long spears or lances, while the Huns were armed with bows.

Gothic horseman

9

Celts

The Celts opposed the landings of the Romans in Britain. They loved fighting, and every Celt was expected to defend his home. They used two-wheeled war chariots pulled by small, fast horses. These chariots were made of wood and had twelve-spoked wheels which had iron rims. Each chariot had two low wooden or wickerwork sides with iron handrails. The driver had a seat but the warrior stood. He wore a bronze breastplate and a bronze helmet, and he carried javelins, an iron sword in a bronze scabbard, and a bronze shield.

The drivers first drove the chariots up and down in front of the enemy while the warriors hurled javelins. Then they drove at the enemy. The warriors jumped down and fought, using their iron swords. The chariots were driven away to the fringe of the battlefield where the drivers waited.

Footsoldiers carried only a spear and a shield. These were given to every Celtic

youth when he reached manhood. They wore no body armour but often covered their bodies with a blue dye called woad which they believed had a magical protection.

The Celts never fought as disciplined troops. In open battle they were no match for the Romans. But when they hid in the forests or hills and made sudden attacks they caused the Romans a great deal of trouble.

Celtic Fortresses

Some Celtic chiefs built strong hill-top fortresses. The best known are Hod Hill and Maiden Castle. Around the top of the hill were dug four or five deep ditches which were protected by high earthworks. The entrances were hidden and could be approached only by narrow passages which were overlooked by high banks of earth like small cliffs.

Early Sea Power

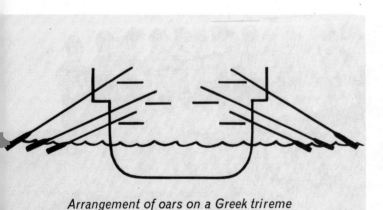

Arrangement of oars on a Greek trireme

Galleys

The value of sea power was quickly appreciated and by 700 B.C. there were special warships. Each warship had a large sail but in battle it was propelled by oars. The captain of the ship tried to snap off the enemy oars and then board the ship, or ram it. A warship had specially strengthened bows.

The Greeks developed the trireme. This was a galley which had three banks of oars on each side of the ship and was rowed by as many as one hundred and seventy men, usually slaves.

The Romans kept a strong fleet to protect the coastline of their Empire. Similar protection was very necessary in Britain. From A.D. 280 the Saxons began to attack Britain. They attacked swiftly up rivers and were away before a detachment of the army could reach them.

Forts were built along the south coast as well as the coasts of Wales and Lancashire, and sea patrols were set up. The patrol boats were sea green to camouflage them. They reported the movements of Saxon ships to the army on shore who either sent a fleet of galleys to intercept them or prepared to meet them on land.

Saxons

The Saxons came from the north west coast of Europe. Ordinary warriors wore no protective clothing except for a leather cap. Their weapon was either a spear about two and three quarters metres long, or a bow and arrows. A chief's leather helmet was covered with bands of metal. It was shaped like a skull cap, although some helmets had neck and cheek guards and some even had a visor. An iron sword was a prized possession and was handed down from father to son.

Some Saxons carried a long, single-edged knife, called a scramasax, which could be over half a metre long. Only a chief wore a mailed shirt. A less common weapon was the axe. This was either a short-handled throwing axe with a curved upturned blade, or a long-handled battle axe which was used in hand-to-hand fighting. Although some Saxons rode horses they dismounted to fight.

axe

throwing axe

scramasax

14

Saxon Shield Wall

The shield played a vital part in a Saxon battle. It was made of wood and was known as an orb. There was an iron boss in the centre. The shield was covered with hide and behind the boss the wood was cut away so that a handgrip could be fitted. Shields were up to three quarters of a metre across.

The warriors lined up shoulder to shoulder so that they presented a wall of shields to the enemy. As the opposing armies advanced, spears, throwing axes and arrows caused much damage. When the two armies met they hacked away with swords, spears and battle-axes.

The Fyrd

When the Saxons settled in Britain the warband chiefs were given land to rule but they stayed at court as the King's bodyguard, and they were his leaders in time of warfare. The ordinary warriors were also given land in return for military service. Land was divided up into hides, and a man who held ten hides was called a thegn. Every free man was expected to leave his land in time of war. The ceorls, or ordinary people, were led in battle by the thegns. This military service was called the fyrd.

The disadvantage of this system became most obvious at the time of King Alfred. The constant raiding by the Vikings meant that an army was needed all the year round. Since most of the fyrd were farmers, their farms were badly neglected.

Alfred's Army

Alfred arranged that only half of the fyrd was called out at one time. A distinction grew up between ceorls who were farmers and only fought when needed, and ceorls who left their land and became professional soldiers at the lord's court. Alfred's army consisted of his own bodyguard or companions, his earls and their companions or retainers, and the fyrd led by his thegns.

The Vikings came from the same coast as the Saxons had come from. Their weapons were the same also. Their sudden up-river attacks were difficult to check. When they raided inland they stole horses so that they could move rapidly.

Burhs

Alfred built a series of fortified towns called burhs where a garrison was kept and where the people could flee for protection. The local people were expected to garrison the burhs. The burhs were able to check the Danish raiders until an armed force could be assembled to deal with them.

Alfred also saw the need for a navy which could intercept the raiders before they landed. He built a fleet of great ships propelled by as many as sixty oars. Free men could be expected to do their fyrd service in the navy.

The Saxon army which faced the Normans at Hastings had changed little from the time of Alfred. It still relied on the fyrd for most of its soldiers. King Harold's own bodyguard, however, was now made up of professional Danish soldiers called 'Housecarls', who wore mailed shirts and helmets, and were armed with huge battle axes.

The Saxon army still fought on foot and depended very much on their shield wall.

The Normans

The Norman army which faced Harold's Saxon army in 1066 contained mounted knights. The Normans, too, were descendants of raiders from North West Europe, but in their fighting against the Franks they had learned the value of heavily armoured cavalry, and by 1066 the Norman knights were the best cavalry in the world.

Each knight wore a mailed shirt called a hauberk, and a helmet. Under the mailed shirt he wore a padded undergarment. He also wore a mailed hood called a coif. He carried a kite-shaped shield, a lance, a sword, and a battle-axe or a mace. The Norman army also contained men-at-arms who carried long spears and swords. There were many archers, too, who fired a one-and-a-half metre long bow. Both archers and men-at-arms wore the mailed shirt and helmet.

First the archers fired volleys of arrows while the men-at-arms attacked to check the enemy until the knights charged.

Knight Service

It was very costly to equip a knight. Besides the cost of his armour and weapons there was the cost of a trained warhorse which had to be strong enough to charge at full gallop carrying a knight in complete armour. The food for the horses was also costly, especially in winter.

The King gave grants of land to his noblemen or barons, who, in return, promised to provide a fixed number of properly trained and equipped knights. At first the barons hired the number of knights they needed, but soon they gave grants from their lands to knights, who provided themselves with arms, armour and warhorses, and promised to serve their lords. Each knight had to serve his lord for forty days each year. If there was no warfare he spent his forty days on garrison duty in a castle, or waiting on his lord.

Motte and Bailey castle

Castles

The Normans were castle builders. Castles were strong points where a garrison could be protected from sudden attacks. Castles were used to keep the country peaceful. During a revolt the garrison could stay in the castle until reinforcements arrived.

Motte and Bailey Castles

The first Norman Castles were Motte and Bailey Castles. The Motte was a mound of earth about twenty-two metres across and fifteen metres high, surrounded by a ditch. On the Motte was a wooden tower called a keep and round it was a wooden stockade. The keep was the home for the family. The ground in front of the Motte was called the Bailey, and this was protected by another stockade and ditch. The entrance was across a drawbridge of planks. Wood was not a good material for the stockade as it caught fire easily and it rotted in wet weather. Suitable stone, when available, was used for the stockade.

Plan

Remains of the 11th-century shell keep at Restormel in Cornwall

Shell Keep

The wooden keep was replaced by a circular stone wall which went right round the top of the Motte. This was called a shell keep. The family lived in buildings in the Bailey, and used the keep only when the castle was under attack.

Stone Keep

The next development was to build a high stone tower, or keep, in the centre of the bailey. The first towers were square, like the Tower of London, but the corners were weak points where attackers could break in, so later towers were round. Some towers were over twenty-seven metres high. The ground floor was left as a store place and the family lived on the first floor. A flight of steps led to the entrance. The stone wall round the Bailey was called a curtain wall. The entrance at the draw-bridge was protected by an outwork or Porch called a Barbican. There was also a portcullis. Slits in the walls enabled defenders to fire in safety on attackers.

Improved castles led to improved siege

weapons. Attackers tried to fill in the moats so that they could push siege towers against the walls. Scaling ladders were still used. Weapons like catapults, ballista, trebuchet and mangonels hurled boulders at the defenders. Sappers dug holes under the walls to try to make the foundations collapse.

Concentric Castles

Once inside the walls any keep could be captured eventually, so castle designers tried to make it more difficult to reach the keep. One way was to build two sets of curtain walls. Each wall had its own towers, ditch and barbican. Every approach to the castle was commanded by loopholes. Some castles had as many as seven portcullises. These castles were called concentric castles. Harlech Castle is a good example of this type of castle.

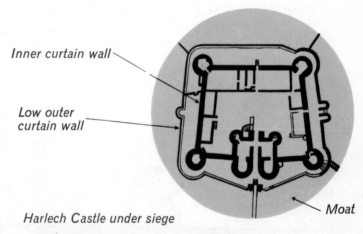

Inner curtain wall

Low outer curtain wall

Moat

Harlech Castle under siege

23

A castle which had strong, natural defences did not need concentric walls. Conway Castle was built on top of a high rock. It had eight strong towers linked by one curtain wall. Siege weapons could not be brought close to the walls because of the sheer slope, and sappers could not dig into the rock.

Castles became so strong that only a siege of many months could capture them. Pitched battles were rare, as armies retreated within the castle walls. If a battle took place knights fought on foot, but the idea was to capture the enemy for ransom. Knights fought in tournaments to maintain their skill.

Conway Castle as it stands today

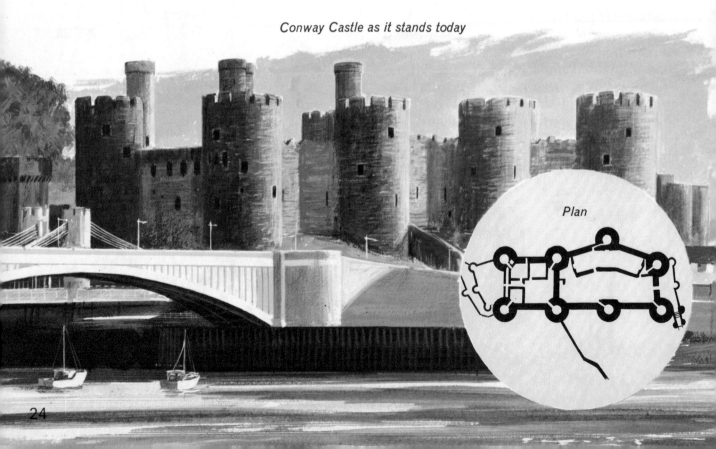

Plan

Middle Ages

Changes in Armour

By 1215 the conical helmet had been replaced by a round, flat-topped steel box which enclosed the head. Under it a knight wore a mail hood. Mail shirts were tunic length and mailed trousers were worn. Shields were smaller and often had a design so that the knight could be recognised, even though his face was hidden. After the Crusades knights wore a linen robe called a surcoat over their armour.

As warfare expanded and campaigns were longer, kings found that the forty day limit to a knight's service was too restricting. One way of overcoming this difficulty was to ask the barons to send half their quota of knights to serve twice as long.

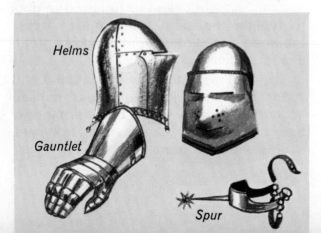

Helms

Gauntlet

Spur

Plate Armour

Some knights preferred to pay a tax called scutage. This was the money required to equip and pay one knight. With the money the king could hire professional knights who served for as long as they were required. For two centuries the mailed knights were the élite of the battlefield. During the fourteenth and fifteenth centuries plate armour gradually replaced mail. This was so heavy that only a special warhorse or destrier could carry a fully armoured knight.

The expense of equipping knights was so heavy that they formed only a small part of the army. In 1242 Edward I's army had only one thousand six hundred knights to twenty thousand footsoldiers. A dismounted knight often commanded a group of footsoldiers.

The fyrd was still part of the army and every free man had to equip himself according to his wealth. Every army now had its sappers, engineers, carpenters, smiths and armourers.

Archers

It was during the fourteenth century that the English longbow emerged as a powerful weapon. At Crecy, Poitiers, and Agincourt the English archers, backed by dismounted men-at-arms, destroyed the flower of French knighthood.

The medieval army now had three parts —

(a) The destructive power of the archers.

(b) The defensive power of the men-at-arms.

(c) The offensive power of the mounted troops.

Early Cannon

Cannon began to appear on the battlefield in the fourteenth century. Edward II used 'gonnes' at the siege of Berwick in 1333 and also at the siege of Calais. The first guns were called 'Pots de fer' and were shaped like vases. The early cannon were crude and unreliable. They were metal tubes into which gunpowder was poured. Then a stone ball or a large arrow was put in and the powder lit through a touch-hole. Often the guns had metal bands round them to make them stronger.

Special short-barrelled cannon, called bombards, were used to fire huge stone balls at castle walls.

Cannon were used on the battlefield but their chief use was against castle or city walls. By 1415 brass cannon were in use which could hurl a 90-kilogramme stone ball. For mobility the cannon were carried on waggons, but by the end of the fifteenth century cannon had their own gun carriages. The barrels could be elevated and metal was used for cannon balls.

Cannon improved very slowly because of the difficulty in producing barrels strong enough without making the guns too heavy to move. In the 1520's a coarser gunpowder, which burned quickly, fired cannon balls farther. Iron cannon were cheaper than bronze ones but were very heavy and brittle.

Gustavus Adolphus

At the beginning of the seventeenth century a Swedish King, Gustavus Adolphus, recognised the importance of field artillery. His field guns were lighter, shorter barrelled, and more mobile. They could be pulled by one horse or three men. Besides firing cannon balls they fired many musket balls called grape shot. By 1800 every army had its heavy siege artillery as well as its field artillery.

Gun on carriage

Early gun waggon

Bombard

Light
horse drawn gun

28

The Arquebus

The first handguns were called arquebuses. The first arquebuses needed two men to fire them because they were so heavy, but in the fifteenth century the arquebus's weight was reduced and one man could support it against his shoulder. This handgun was a simple hollow tube down which powder and shot were rammed. There was a hole in the side or top of the tube called the touch hole. The powder was lit by a piece of fibre called a match.

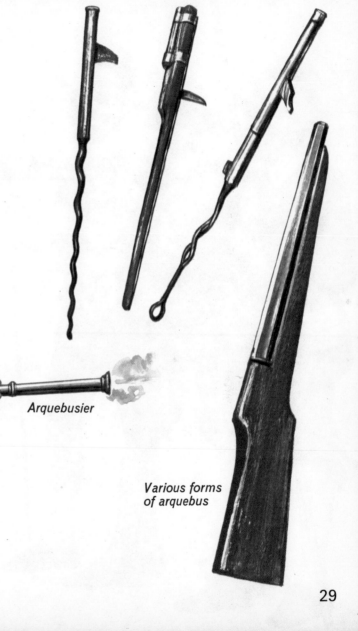

Arquebusier

Various forms of arquebus

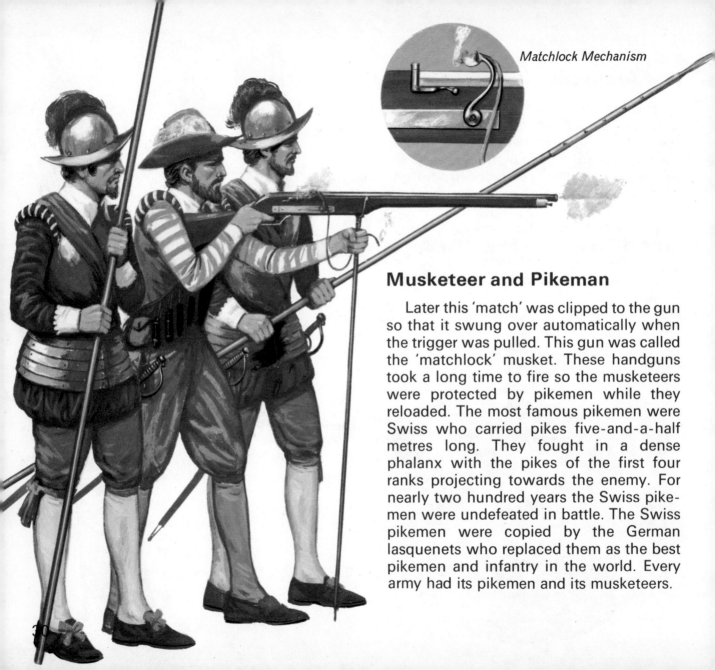

Matchlock Mechanism

Musketeer and Pikeman

Later this 'match' was clipped to the gun so that it swung over automatically when the trigger was pulled. This gun was called the 'matchlock' musket. These handguns took a long time to fire so the musketeers were protected by pikemen while they reloaded. The most famous pikemen were Swiss who carried pikes five-and-a-half metres long. They fought in a dense phalanx with the pikes of the first four ranks projecting towards the enemy. For nearly two hundred years the Swiss pikemen were undefeated in battle. The Swiss pikemen were copied by the German lasquenets who replaced them as the best pikemen and infantry in the world. Every army had its pikemen and its musketeers.

Flintlock and Bayonet

In the sixteenth century the matchlock was replaced by the 'wheel-lock'. Each musket had a priming pan which contained the gun powder. The hammer of the musket was called the cock. This cock was armed with pyrites which rubbed against a ribbed wheel. When the trigger was pulled sparks came from the pyrites to light the powder and fire the gun.

The next development was the 'flintlock'. When the trigger was pulled a piece of flint struck sparks into the priming pan. This musket was standard equipment until 1815. The English infantry musket was known as 'Brown Bess'.

Towards the end of the seventeenth century the socket bayonet and ring bayonet were invented. The ring bayonet could be fitted over the barrel of the musket so that infantry could defend themselves against cavalry, and no longer needed pikemen to protect them. Infantry now had greater mobility.

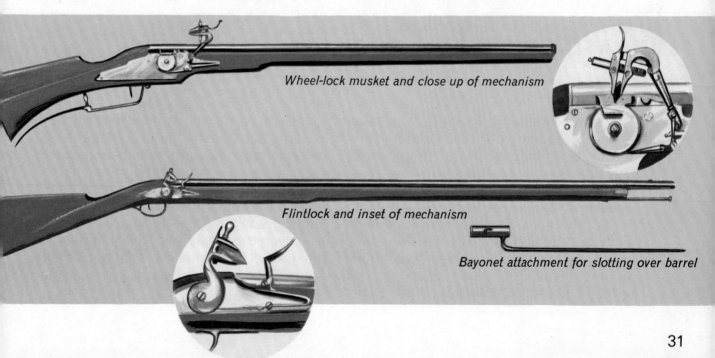

Wheel-lock musket and close up of mechanism

Flintlock and inset of mechanism

Bayonet attachment for slotting over barrel

Fortresses

Section showing fortress, ditch and earth ramparts

Gun Forts

The development of cannon and muskets affected the whole tactics of warfare, especially when fortresses were involved. The high castle wall was an easy target for gunners. In front of a sixteenth century fortress a rampart of earth was built to protect the guns. Behind this was a deep ditch, and behind this was the stone wall which projected only a few feet above ground level. Protecting parts, called bastions, protected the walls on each side.

Since stone shattered when hit by a cannon ball most of the defence works were of packed earth. Sharpened stakes protected the earth ramparts and prevented infantry from storming them. The bastions were round at first but this left too many 'blind' spots on the walls, which could not be covered by firearms. The ramparts for the guns of the fortresses were open to the air so that their fumes could easily escape.

Vauban

Rounded bastions were replaced by angled ones and fortresses were designed so that guns could be brought to bear on an enemy, no matter in which direction he approached. There was also a curtain defence of earthworks where infantry could fire at anyone approaching.

In the seventeenth century a French engineer, called Vauban, brought this type of fortress to perfection.

Attackers had to adopt new tactics. The open ground was too dangerous and so zigzag trench systems were dug to get as close to the walls as possible ready for an assault. Sappers who dug the trenches were protected by wicker cylinders, filled with earth, called gabions. Vauban was also an expert at besieging fortresses. He thought of the ricochet shot. This could be used by firing a gun with a reduced amount of powder so that the shot lobbed over the defences.

Vauban type fortress

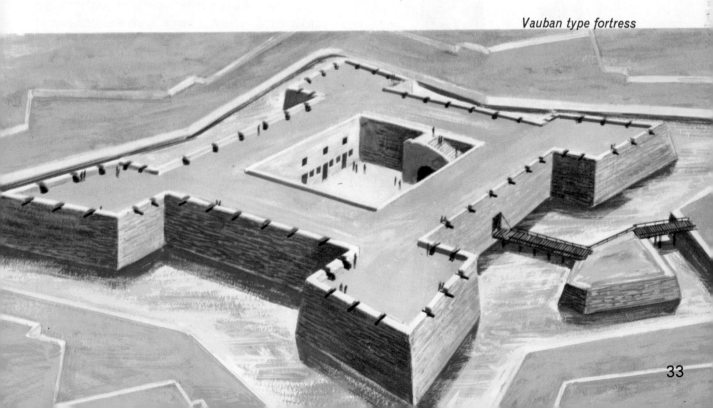

Cavalry

Mounted soldiers were also affected by the new weapons. Heavy armour was no longer sufficient protection, and body armour, except for a breastplate, was discarded. This gave them greater mobility.

Reiters

Royalist Cavalry

Reiters

The German heavy cavalry were called 'Reiters'. During the Thirty Years War 1618–48 they were equipped with pistols. They moved forward in ranks at a walk. The first rank then charged and fired their pistols at the enemy and then wheeled away to reload. The second rank followed, then the third, and so on until the first rank were ready again.

Gustavus armed his cavalry with sword and pistol. They charged at the enemy at full gallop.

Ironsides

During the Civil War in Britain Prince Rupert, the Royalists' cavalry commander, also used the full charge. They carried everything before them until Oliver Cromwell trained his Ironsides. The Ironsides were armed with a carbine, two pistols and a sword. They wore a back and front breastplate and a helmet. They charged at the trot, keeping perfect line.

Dragoons

Another type of mounted soldier was the dragoon. He was armed with a musket but, although he rode into battle, he dismounted to fight.

Cavalryman

Ileryman

Pikeman

Professional Soldiers

From the fourteenth century the type of soldier had changed. Professional soldiers, like the Swiss pikemen and German lasquenets, fought for anyone who would pay them. Each country began to depend more and more on a regular army. During the sixteenth century Gustavus Adolphus's idea of giving troops uniforms was copied by every country.

Red Coats

The New Model Army which the Parliamentary forces raised in 1645 was the first real British Army. It was divided into Cavalry, Dragoons, Artillery and Infantry. The infantry were given red uniforms which was to be the dress of British Infantry until the end of the nineteenth century.

Eighteenth Century

During the eighteenth century, under the influence of commanders like Marlborough, Fredrick the Great, Napoleon and Wellington, armies of the world took on a modern look. Noblemen raised regiments of soldiers. Young men who could afford it bought commissions and became officers, while ordinary men enlisted for a period of years.

Trained Infantry

The infantry were drilled and drilled. They were trained to form hollow squares to withstand cavalry. When attacking, British Infantry advanced in two long lines which gave greater fire power. They were trained to fire, one rank at a time, in volleys. A trained infantryman could now fire two rounds a minute.

Improved Artillery

Artillery could keep pace with the infantry. Jean de Maritz had developed a new way of boring cannon which made the barrel stronger. Guns were lighter and could be easily drawn by horses. Coke smelting of iron made improved cheaper iron guns. Gun carriages ran more smoothly. Every army now included many guns.

Specialised Troops

Supporting the main infantry were specialist troops, the light infantry and the grenadiers. These were the storm troopers who led the attack on fortifications. Many of the light infantry were riflemen. The rifle had a special groove in the barrel which made the bullet spin and thus travel more accurately. They advanced in open order, sniping and skirmishing. The riflemen's uniform was green with dark buttons so that they were camouflaged.

Originally the grenadiers threw hand bombs called grenades which were lit by hand before they were thrown. Although the grenadiers retained their name, they became part of the general infantry and carried rifles.

Heavy and Light Cavalry

Cavalry, too, was divided into different sections. The light cavalry, or Hussars, were used as skirmishers, harassing enemy supply wagons and escorting their own supply wagons. They also led the chase when an enemy broke and ran. The Austrians equipped some Hussar regiments with lances, and soon all armies had their lancer regiments.

The heavy cavalry rode powerful horses.

They were armed with large cavalry swords and some wore breastplates. They made massive charges at enemy infantry or guns. The dragoons became part of the heavy cavalry.

Soldiers of the Rifle Brigade and Highland Light Infantry

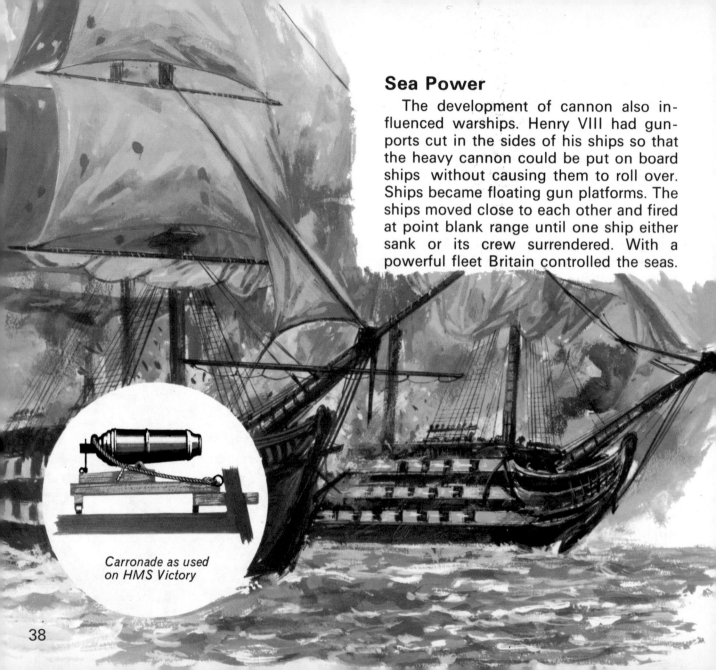

Sea Power

The development of cannon also influenced warships. Henry VIII had gunports cut in the sides of his ships so that the heavy cannon could be put on board ships without causing them to roll over. Ships became floating gun platforms. The ships moved close to each other and fired at point blank range until one ship either sank or its crew surrendered. With a powerful fleet Britain controlled the seas.

Carronade as used on HMS Victory

Nineteenth Century and
Twentieth Century

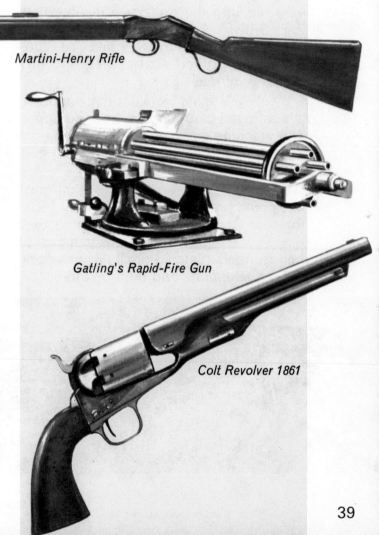

Martini-Henry Rifle

Improved Rifles

In 1839 the breech-loading rifle was invented. The French adopted the Chasse-pot rifle and in 1871 the British Army adopted the Martini-Henry rifle. The first repeater rifle which had a magazine to hold ten bullets was developed in 1898, and the Colt revolver, which fired six rounds, was invented by Samuel Colt in 1832. Infantry could now fire so rapidly that attack was very costly. This was especially so when machine guns were developed.

Automatic Weapons

The first effective machine gun was invented by Richard Gatling, an American, in 1862. This had a number of barrels fastened together. A container above the gun fed in cartridges. The gunner turned a handle and the rotating barrels fired in turn. This gun could fire six hundred rounds a minute.

Gatling's Rapid-Fire Gun

Colt Revolver 1861

In 1883 Hiram S. Maxim designed the first modern machine gun. It had a water jacket to keep the barrel cool. The bullets were fed into the gun by a flexible belt. The British Army adopted a Maxim machine gun which weighed 18 kilogrammes and fired six hundred and fifty rounds a minute.

By 1900 most armies had adopted camouflaged clothing and were equipped with machine guns, rifles, heavy and light artillery. During the 1914–18 War steel helmets were again worn.

Guns were now so powerful that gunners could fire at targets which they could not see. Observation Officers, sited well in front of the guns, used flags to signal to their gunners. Later, signalling was done by field telephone and then by radio.

Heavy Howitzer of 1st World War

Maxim Machine gun

18 pounder of the 1st World War

Modern 105 mm Howitzer

Aircraft

During the twentieth century, war in the air was developed. The artillery realised the value of observation from the air. First the Observation Officer used a captive balloon, and later he worked from aircraft. The use of aircraft increased rapidly. Fighter aircraft protected observer aircraft. Bombers flew over enemy lines, while Zeppelins and heavy bombers attacked cities and supply lines.

Tanks

Because the opposing armies were deeply entrenched, protected by barbed wire entanglements, and backed by the firepower of their weapons, the infantry attack in mass was a failure. The deadlock was broken by the tank, a British invention. The first tank was called 'Little Willie'. It had its trials in 1915 but it was a failure. In February 1916 'Big Willie', or 'Mother' as it came to be known, was tested. It was able to cross a three metre wide trench and climb a one-and-a-half metre breastwork. It had a crew of eight and was armed with two 'six-pounder' guns and four machine guns. The first 'Mothers' were shipped to France in crates labelled 'Water tanks'.

By 1939 tanks were used by all armies. They replaced the cavalry. Light tanks took the place of light cavalry for scouting, and heavy tanks replaced heavy cavalry for frontal attacks. The development of the tank led to the invention of anti-tank guns and anti-tank mines. Special tanks called 'funnies' were used in the Second World War. Flail tanks disposed of mines, while bridging tanks laid bridges. D.D. tanks, which could travel for six-and-a-half kilometres underwater, were used for landing on beaches.

Airpower, too, continued to develop. The Germans used the blitz-krieg attack, which was an attack led by tanks and dive-bombers supported by motorised infantry in lorries. Special anti-aircraft guns were needed to deal with air attack. The mobility of this form of attack exposed the weakness of fortified strong points.

A Flail Tank

The Tetrarch light tank of the 2nd World War

Chieftain tank of the present day

Fortresses

*Maginot line
Inset shows turret
and lift*

The Last of the Great Fortresses

It had been realised that even the massive fortresses of Vauban were no longer impregnable against the firepower of artillery. The enemy guns had to be kept as far away as possible from the main fort, so a ring of smaller forts and strong points had been built around the main defence.

Defence guns, too, had to be re-sited. They were too exposed on open parapets. The guns were put in steel turrets which were protected by thick concrete. A Belgian, Brailment, designed a turret which could be raised and lowered, so that it could emerge to fire then sink from view when not in use. The gaps between the forts were filled with trenches and strong points. The Maginot Line and the Siegfried Line were built on this idea. A line of heavily protected forts was linked by trenches, minefields, tank traps and barbed wire.

But the mobility of the German army in 1939 proved that a line of fortifications was no longer a reliable defence.

Nuclear-powered submarine

Aircraft carrier

Battleship

Guided Missile Destroyer

Modern Naval Warfare

Steam Warships

Naval tactics changed little until the invention of the steam ship and high explosive shells. Ships were first armoured with steel plate and then they were built entirely of steel. Guns were placed in movable turrets on the deck of the ship to give them a wider range of fire. Special tracking equipment was necessary to fire guns accurately over distances of several kilometres.

Submarines

The development of the submarine affected naval strategy. Submarines could sink ships without even surfacing. Special ships were developed to fight this new menace with specialised tracking equipment to find submarines and drop depth charges on them.

The Second World War ended the era of the large battleship when aircraft, launched from aircraft carriers, proved how vulnerable they were to air attack.

Guided Missile Ships

The navy today concentrates on aircraft carriers, backed by a fleet of smaller guided missile ships and atomic powered submarines.

The Army Today

*Guided missile
on launching platform*

*Radar Control System for
locating enemy mortar positions*

Guided Missiles

The modern army relies on mobility and firepower with co-ordination between tanks, infantry, aircraft and artillery. The most modern artillery is the guided missile with an atomic warhead. The gun is just a launching platform for the rocket, which is guided to its target by radar.

The infantry are all equipped with automatic repeating rifles. They have small guided missiles which can be fired by one man, and which are used as anti-tank weapons, capable of penetrating the thickest armour plating.

No longer does the strength of an army depend on the number of men. With modern weapons the requirement is a smaller force of highly-trained specialised troops. The modern soldier must be able to handle automatic weapons, electric and electronic equipment and radar, as well as having a wide range of engineering skill.

Horsa glider of the 2nd World War

Paratrooper

Commando

Commandos

Special mobility in the modern army is provided by the commando troops. These troops are trained to exercise initiative, and to attack quickly. They are chosen for their toughness, self-reliance and bravery. They are trained to scale cliffs, and find their way in enemy occupied country. They are taught unarmed combat, close fighting using grenades and knives, and how to use explosives. Commandos land on beaches, quickly do as much damage as possible, and are away before the enemy can recover from their surprise.

Airborne Troops

Airborne troops are also commandos. They land by parachute or from large, towed gliders to disrupt enemy communications or seize bridges before an advance, or capture strong points which could hold up an advance.

Engineers

An army, of course, needs more than fighting troops. The Royal Engineers, the descendants of the Sappers and Miners of the Middle Ages, dig mines, clear land-mines by using mine detectors, and disarm unexploded bombs. They build roads and bridges.

Auxiliary Troops

The Royal Corps of Transport supplies the army with fuel and food.

The Royal Army Ordnance Corps provides it with weapons, equipment and ammunition.

The Corps of Royal Electrical and Mechanical Engineers keeps the equipment in good order.

Communications are handled by the Royal Corps of Signals, and the sick and wounded are cared for by the Royal Army Medical Corps.

The Military Police control traffic and Padres take care of the troops' spiritual welfare. Further education is organised by the Royal Army Education Corps.

Women Soldiers

There are women, too, in the modern army who do many jobs besides nursing. The W.R.A.C. drive lorries, ambulances and cars. They work as secretaries, typists, clerks and storekeepers. They operate radio, telephone and electrical and electronic equipment, as well as being expert caterers and cooks.

INDEX